Lamps of the 50s & 60s

Jan Lindenberger

Revised & Expanded 2nd Edition

Schiffer Publishing Ltd

4880 Lower Valley Road, Atglen, PA 19310 USA

Revised price guide: 2004

Library of Congress Control Number: 2004101492

Type set in Korinna BT
Designed by Laurie Smucker

ISBN: 0-7643-2069-6
Printed in China
1 2 3 4

Published by Schiffer Publishing Ltd.
4880 Lower Valley Road
Atglen, PA 19310
Phone: (610) 593-1777; Fax: (610) 593-2002; E-mail: Info@schifferbooks.com
Please visit our web site catalog at
www.schifferbooks.com

In Europe, Schiffer books are distributed by
Bushwood Books
6 Marksbury Avenue
Kew Gardens
Surrey TW9 4JF England
Phone: 44 (0) 20-8392-8585; Fax: 44 (0) 20-8392-9876; E-mail: info@bushwoodbooks.co.uk
Free postage in the UK. Europe: air mail at cost.

Contents

Acknowledgments

A very special thank you to Myke Johnson from 50/Fiftys Antiques for allowing me to come to her home to photograph her vast collection. The majority of the lamps in this book are from her shop and her home. Myke deals in 50s/60s collectibles and furniture. Her patience in arranging and rearranging her home is greatly appreciated. Another special thanks to Bill and Kristi Lewis for the large contribution from their home and shop, Spotlight on Modern, in the Antique Center, Denver, Colorado. Also thanks to Doni Brune for her special added touch. An to anyone else whom I may have forgotten.

50/Fifty featured at Mountain Man Antiques, Denver, Colorado
Antique Mart of Elk Grove, Illinois
Bill and Kristi Lewis, Spotlight on Modern, Denver, Colorado
American Classics Antique Mall, Colorado Springs, Colorado
De'Ja'Vu, St. Joseph, Missouri
Magpie Antiques, Elk Grove, Illinois
Your Quest Ends Here Antique Mall, Granger, Indiana
Johnnie Mae Gipe, St. Joseph, Missouri
Darlene Schaake, Antique Center on Broadway, Denver, Colorado
Bill Kieffert, Denver, Colorado
Tammie and Roger Sawicki, Denver, Colorado
Top Value Stamp Catalog. Top Value Enterprises, Inc. N.Y., N.Y. 1956
Living Magazine. September, 1961, N.Y., N.Y.
Spiegel Catalog. Spring & summer, 1962. Chicago, Ill.
Montgomery Ward Catalog. 1969. Kansas City, Mo.

Introduction

You light up my life!

What can one say about these lamps that are "so bad, they're good?"

Chances are, you will recognize quite a few of these kitchy items from the 1940s through the early 1970s and wonder what ever inspired anyone to design, let alone buy and decorate their homes with these lamps.

While the utility of a lamp in the home is quite obvious, design and decorating are something else again. The thoroughly modern 1950s housewife, wanting to implement art and modern design into her household, found a natural outlet for this urge in lighting. Designers offered all manner of scientific patterns such as amoeba, starburst, and atomic styles to reflect the postwar mood. Additionally, new materials and production techniques developed during the war era were readily available for new commercial purposes. All of these forces collided to create the lamps we hate to love. But love them we do. How could we pass up a "Rembrandt," with its stylized shade atop a brass ball trapped in a black steel base? To us, these lamps represent an era of hope, modernism, and faith that science and technology had stepped in to create a bright future for the hardworking American family.

Take the T.V. lamp for example. Born of the concern over eyesight damage from the modern contraption which so fascinated the American family, the T.V. lamp sought to alleviate middle class discomfort about the dangers of television viewing. Taking advantage of television's new flat surface, no ethnic group or member of the animal kingdom was overlooked by the modern housewife with a flair for decorating. You could visit the depths of the ocean, darkest Africa, or far away China, simply by turning on your T.V. lamp that doubled as a planter. And some planter T.V. lamps even came with a package of planter mix. Adding to the proliferation of T.V. lamps, many companies threw in a lamp with the purchase of a new television set.

Not content with stationary T.V. lamps, the action lamp was resurrected for those who desired a little more excitement in the living room decor. Action lamps had been around since the 1920s, depicting such scenes as Niagara Falls, forest fires, trains, and buses, Hopalong Cassidy, from the 1950s, is among the most valuable and sought after of these lamps. Other popular novelty lamps of the era include fish bowl styles, motorized hula dancers, angel fish swimming around a clock face. A truly kitchy example has to be the phone-clock-cigarette lighter combination with venetian blind shade.

For a "blast from the past" we always enjoy a 1960s cult favorite, the Lava Lite. The advertisement for the classic Century model promised a "motion for every emotion." The Century is still being produced today, but the older originals can be identified by the screw-on caps. For fun, hippies also indulged themselves with the rarer Spaceship, Aladdin-style and Coach Lantern lamps too. Not to be left out, the Japanese even got in on the fad with a highly collectible cylindrical T.V. lamp knockoff of the Lava Lite.

Today, lamps are fun collectibles, relatively inexpensive and easy to find, and they can add a humorous touch to any decorating scheme. The examples in this book are some of the best (and worst) we could dig up, but there are hundreds of styles out there to light up your life. We hope this book will "turn you on" to lamps.

I hope you take this lamp handbook and price guide, with you on your lamp buying trips and use it to find just the right light!

Prices are based upon my personal observations and may differ from coast to coast. Auction prices may differ from shop prices. Prices are also affected by condition and availability.

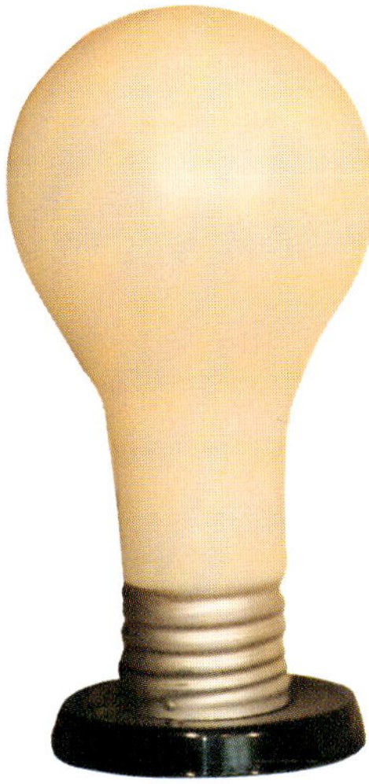

Table Lamps

Brass, Metal, & Wood

Ceramic and brass with fiberglass shade and starburst bulb. $150-200

Brass designers table lamp with fiberglass shades. 24". $100-175

Brass and wood bommerang lamp with fiberglass shade. $100-150

Metal table lamp with glass center insert. 26". $50-75

Wood and brass bommerang lamp with fiberglass shade. 26". $150-250 pair

Brass S-shaped table lamp with double fiberglass shades. $100-150

Polished brass table lamp with half moon-shaped wood design and fiberglass leaf shape shade. $150-250

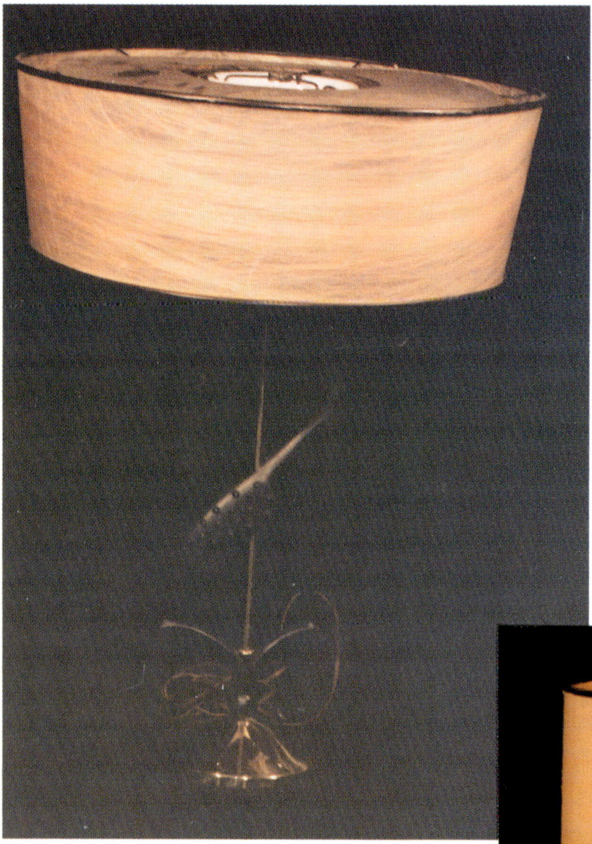

Spun fiberglass shade on metal poles and base. Table lamp. 60". $100-125

Metal spiral table lamp with cardboard shade. 24"-30". $75-150

Wooden design with marble base. 22". $60-75

Brass and painted metal table lamp, plastic flowers in base with fiberglass shade. 31". $75-100

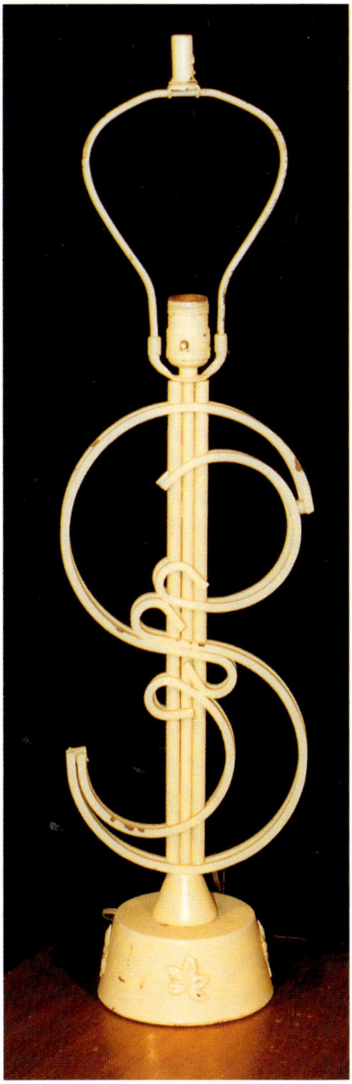

Iron dollar sign lamp. 18". $50-75

Brass table lamp. $60-75

Wood and brass table lamp with cloth shades. $75-100

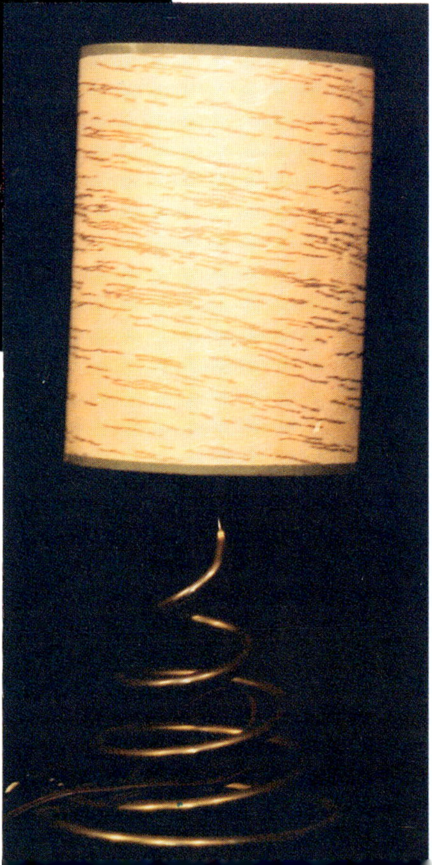

Brass spiral table lamp with cardboard shade. $40-50

Black and brass base with white veiling fiberglass shade. Oxford. 17". $60-75. Top Value stamp catalog, no. 22-50.

Palm table lamp with fiberglass shade. 40". $250-450 pair

Wooden designer's table lamp. 40". Fiberglass shade. 27". $60-75

Wooden table lamp. $75-100

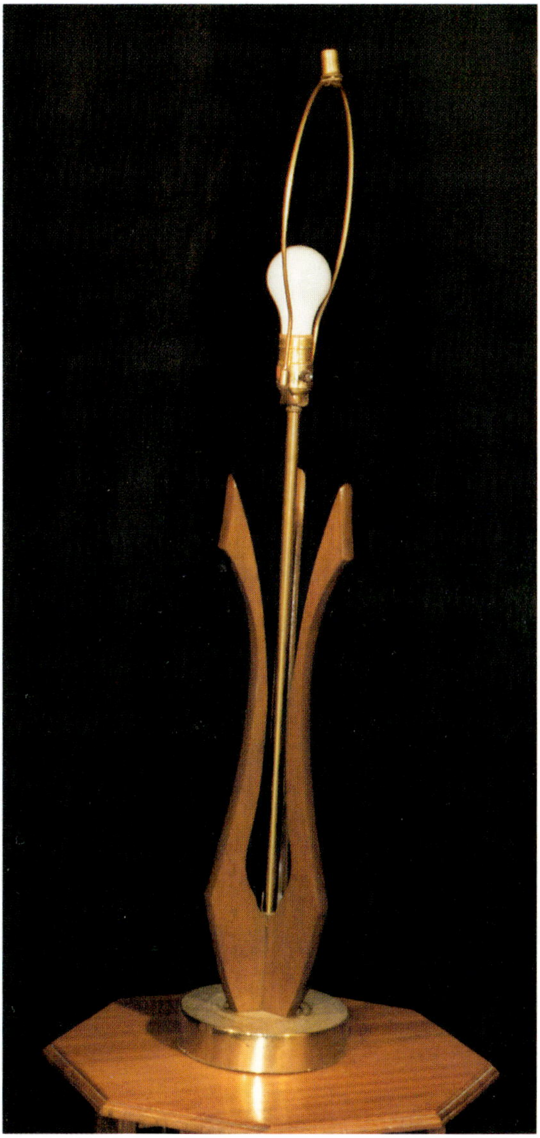

Wood table lamp. 18". $40-60

Wood with metal base table lamp. Atomic design on top. 21". $100-125 pair

Wood and brass bommerang lamp with double fiberglass shade. 30". $100-175

Black metal wing design table lamp. 16". $30-45

Pink fiberglass shade on brass spiral lamp. 25". $150-250

Brass double table lamp with fiberglass shades. $45-65

Table lamp with green glass design and brass spindles. Fiberglass shade. 33". $150-200 each

Clear glass table lamp with cardboard shade. Gold fish design. 31". $100-200 each. $200-400 pair

Ceramic and brass table lamp with Venetian blind shade. 22". $50-75

Gold trimmed plaster table lamp. Fiberglass dimensional shade. 28". $60-75

Brass and iron table lamp. Rembrandt Masterpiece Lamps. 29".
$125-150 pair

Ceramic light pink swirl lamp with gold fleck. Wire pleated shade. 26". $30-40

Ceramic lamp with fiberglass shades. $150-175

Ceramic T.V. lamp with fiberglass shade. 28". $150-175

Plaster lamp with fiberglass tiered shade, starburst light bulbs. 16". $75-125

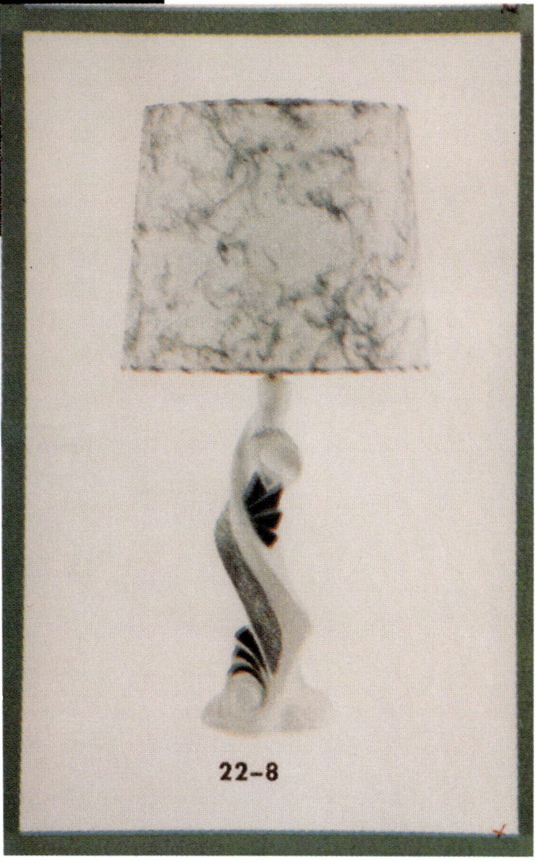

Plastic and ceramic designer's lamp with fiberglass shade. 31.5". $75-125. Top Value stamp catalog, no. 22-8. 1956.

Ceramic table lamp with two-tier fiberglass shade. 27". $150-175 pr.

Ceramic feather design table lamp. 32". $60-75

Ceramic table lamp with fiberglass shade. 24". $130-150 pair

Ceramic turquoise and gold leaf lamp with two tier fiberglass shade. 26". $100-150 pair

Fiberglass swirl shade with base of plaster. Bulbs strut out from sides. 28". $40-50

Ceramic table lamp in a driftwood style with cloth shade. 26". $65-85

Ceramic table lamp with two-tier fiberglass shade. Plasto Mf'g Co. 27". $75-95 pair

Ceramic horse shoe-shape lamp. Paper shade. 14". $125-150 pair

Ceramic ballet dancer lamp with the wrong shade. 20". $50-75

Ceramic Victorian couple table lamp. The shade is wrong. 26". $75-100

Ceramic ballet dancers lamp. The shade is not original. $50-75

Fiberglass triple shade table lamp. Lucite base with ceramic revolving lady. Moss. 38". $400-650

Lucite base with fiberglass upper section and shade. $100-200

Lucite floor lamp. Moss. 60". $400-500

Lucite lamps with silk shades. 19". $50-75 each

Lucite table lamp. Moss. 24". $400-600 pair. It came as a three-piece set. 2 table lamps and 1 floor.

Orange paper lantern style T.V. lamp. 16". $20-25

Plastic and wood desk lamp. 15". $20-30

Plastic light bulb table lamp. 23". $100-150

Atomic chrome table lamp. 17". $100-150

Glass ball table lamp. 1970s. 12". $150-275

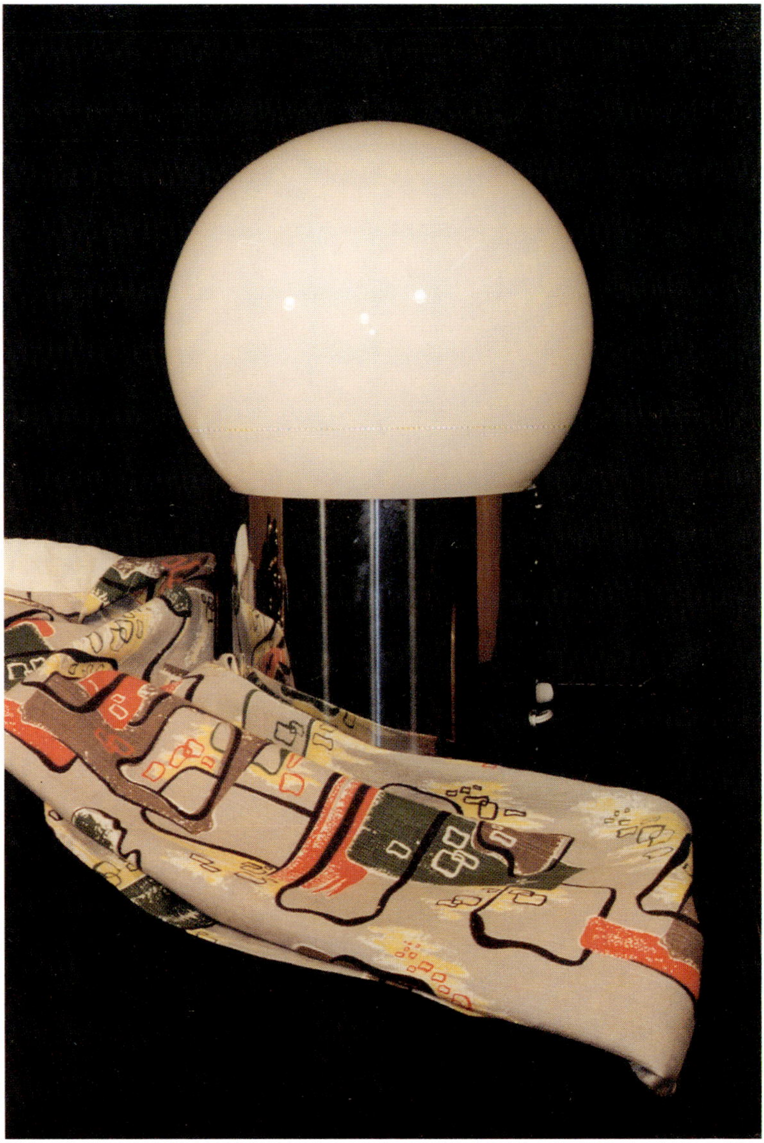

Table lamp with aluminum circular base and glass globe on top. $100-160

Ceramic gazelle table lamp with fiberglass shade. 30". $100-150

Ceramic floral lamp with paper shade. $110-145 pair

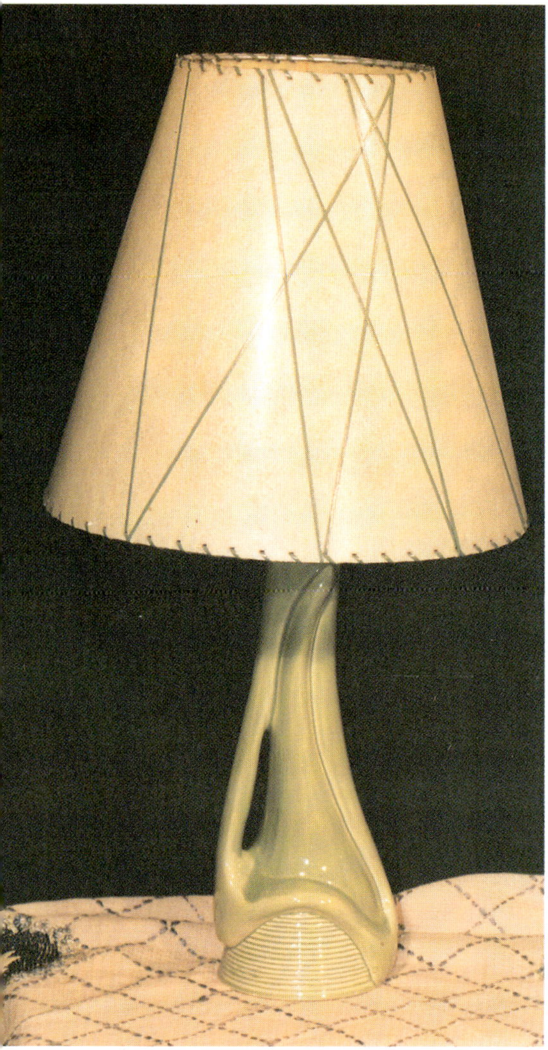

Ceramic table lamp. Fiberglass shade. 32". $50-75

Ceramic green table lamp. (Wrong shade). 14". $30-45

Ceramic oriental style table lamp with fiberglass shade. 26". $125-175 pair

Ceramic table lamp with fiberglass shade. 26". $50-80

Ceramic woman table lamp. $50-85

Ceramic panther lamp with fiberglass shade. 27". $75-100

Ceramic oriental table lamp with fiberglass shade. 26". $50-75

Ceramic basket table lamp/planter. Paper shade. 22". $60-75

Ceramic table lamp with leaf design. Fiberglass shade. 29". $50-75

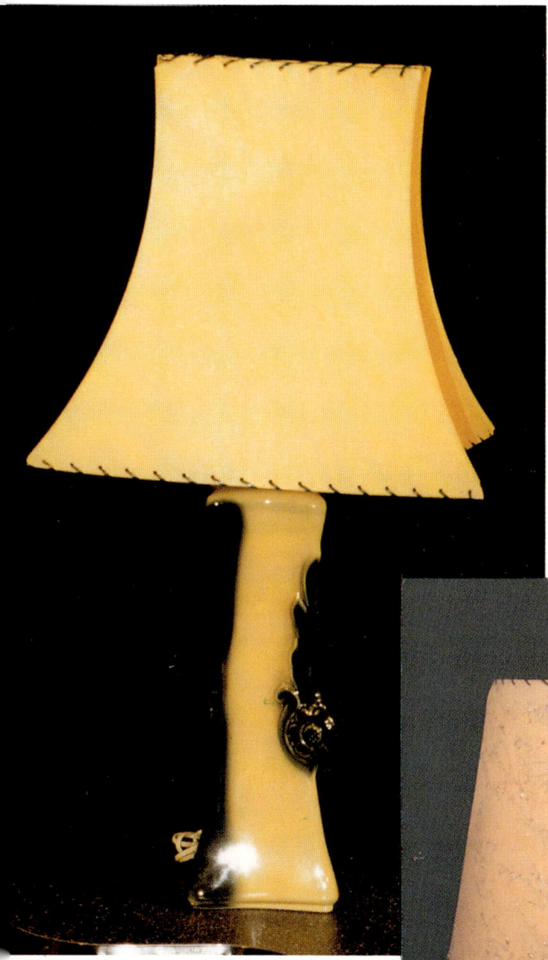

Ceramic table lamp with fiberglass shade. 32". $60-80

Driftwood type ceramic table lamp with fiberglass shade. 30". $60-75

Ceramic table lamp. 8" tall. $20-30

Ceramic cactus table lamp with cone shaped fiberglass shade. 24". $35-55

Ceramic table lamp with floral insert. Fiberglass shade. $50-75

Ceramic pink with gold trim table lamp. Fiberglass pleated shade. 26". $30-40

Ceramic pink and gold table lamp. Fiberglass double circular shade. 27". $30-40

Ceramic and plastic table lamp with fiberglass shade. 26". $50-75

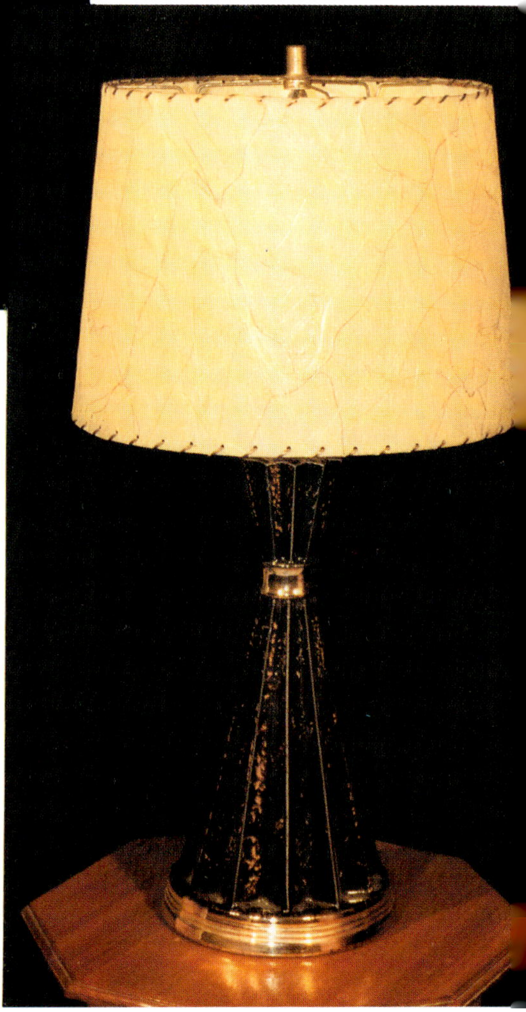

Ceramic gold and black table lamp. Fiberglass shade. $50-75

Brass and ceramic table lamp with two-tier paper shade. 24". $50-75

Black ceramic table lamp with fiberglass shade. 16". $60-75

Plaster table lamp. Geometric shape with wood top. $40-50

Ceramic gold trimmed table lamp. (Wrong shade). 16". $30-45

Ceramic table lamp.
$40-50

Ceramic painted, gold leaf table lamp, with fiberglass shade. 27".
$45-65

China figurine lamp with gold fiberglass shade. 16". $60-75

Ceramic pink table lamp with fiberglass shade. 40". $50-60

Ceramic table lamps with gold accents. Fiberglass shades. 20". $45-60 pair

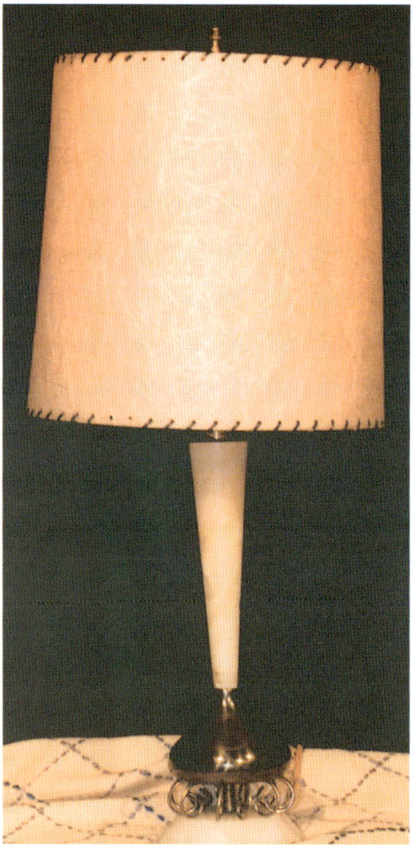

Alabaster and brass table lamp with fiberglass shade. 25". $75-100 pair

Yellow ceramic base lamp with plastic shade. 18". $40-50

Pair of ceramic bedroom lamps. Cardboard shade. 15". $40-60 pair

Ceramic crown T.V. light. 12". $45-65

Ceramic T.V. lamp in metal base which doubles as a planter. $40-60

Dresser lamp in black ceramic with gold swirl. Fiberglass shade. 19". $95-125 pair

Ceramic T.V. lamp with glass flowers. 10". $25-50

Table lamp in gold leaf on clear frosted glass. Silk shade. 36.5". $50-65

Hall china table lamp. Hand painted leaf design on concave china column with a brass base. Rayon shade. 28". $55-75. Top Value stamp catalog. 1956.

Brass base with china flower design on china lamp. Silk shade. Cordey. 29". $45-65. Top Value stamp catalog, no. 22-45.

Glass table lamp. Came as a pair. 21". $120-140 pair

Glass table lamp. Came as a pair. 21". $150-175 pair

Brass lamp with fiberglass shade. Bulbs have plastic spiked covers. 26". $60-75

Etched layered glass table lamp. Silk shade. 40". $50-60

Ceramic column with climbing vine table lamp. Paper pleated shade. 32". $45-60

Hand painted floral glass table lamp with gold accents and brass base. Silk shade. 38". $50-75

Ceramic table lamp with embossed flowers and gold tone base. 26". $40-50

Ceramic table lamp with gold design and trim on brass sculptured base. Paper pleated shade. 29". $40-50

Crystal prisms, with marble and pot metal base table lamp. Silk shade. 44". $125-145

Ceramic panther lamp/ planter with fiberglass shade. 22". $85-125

Glass horses on brass base with glass prisms in the center, T.V. lamp. 11". $75-95

Ceramic panther desk lamp with fiberglass shade. 16". $65-100

Ceramic planter lamp. (Wrong shade). 22". $45-65

Ceramic T.V. lamp of panthers. $75-100

Black panther. T.V. lamp. 1950s. 12". $60-80

Black panther table lamp. 6". $50-75

Ceramic panther T.V. lamp/planter. 10". $40-50

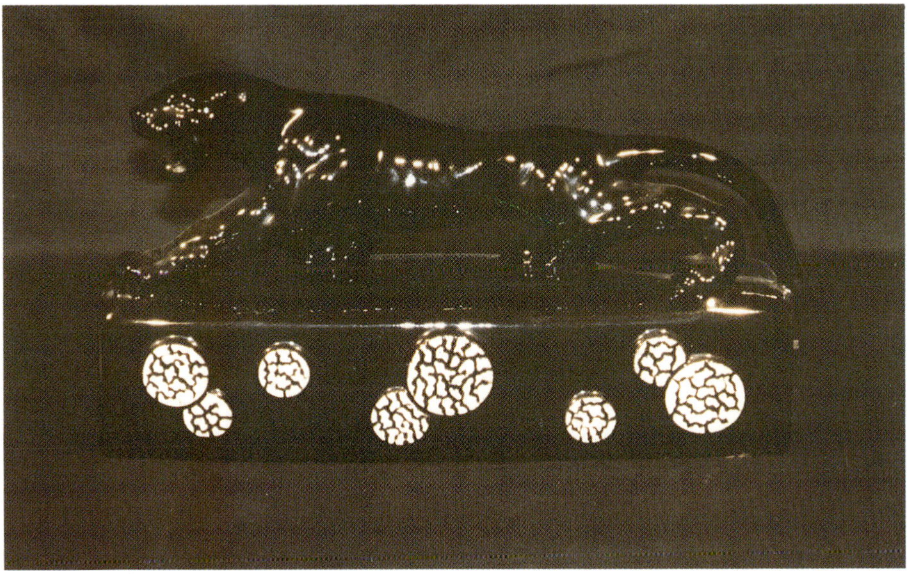

Ceramic panther T.V. lamp. 9". $65-95

Ceramic panther T.V. lamp and planter. 8". $50-75

Ceramic panther T.V. lamp. $45-65

Black ceramic panther with fiberglass shade, T.V. lamp. 10". $60-125

Ceramic boxer T.V. lamp with fiberglass shade. 10". $75-125

Ceramic Dachshund T.V. lamp with fiberglass shade. 10". $75-125

Plaster, dogs, night light. 8". $50-75

Lucite dog with plastic base T.V. lamp. $75-125

Ceramic poodle on wood base T.V. lamp. Fiberglass shade. 12". $75-125

Pair of plaster poodles, table lamps. Fiberglass shades with felt applied poodles that have rhinestone eyes. 24". $200-250 pair

Ceramic horse speckled with gold design T.V. lamp. 12". $50-75

Plaster rearing horse table lamp. 22". $40-60

Phil-Mar horse and foal lamp. Ebony ceramic base. Red fiberglass shade. 25". $55-75. Top Value stamp catalog, no. 22-3. 1956.

Ceramic gazelle table lamp. $45-55

Ceramic deer T.V. lamp with glass insert. 14". $50-75

Ceramic gazelle T.V. lamp/ planter. Fiberglass shade. 26". $75-100

Ceramic gazelle table lamp/planter. (Wrong shade). 14". $40-60

Ceramic fish and sea shell T.V. lamp. $40-60

Plaster fish with glass insert lamp. Fiberglass shade. 31". $100-150

Ceramic fish T.V. lamp with fiberglass shade and ceramic finial fish. 6"-24". $175-325

Ceramic fish T.V. lamp. Lane and Co. Van Ives, Ca. 1957. 14". $75-125

Ceramic sea shell look table lamp with fish swimming around the base. Fiberglass shade. 40". $75-100

Plastic fish T.V. lamp. 8". $50-75

Sea shell lamp with wood base. 8". $20-30

Ceramic deer T.V. lamp. 8". $45-65

Ceramic ram T.V. lamp. 14". $50-75

Ceramic duck T.V. lamp and planter. 12". $40-50

Ceramic flying duck T.V. light. 12". $45-65

Ceramic flying duck T.V. light. 14". $75-100

Sea shell T.V. lamp with beach scene. 8". $50-75

Plaster bird on leaf table lamp. Cloth shade. 27". $75-95

Ceramic swan T.V. lamp. Fiberglass back. 10". $40-55

Ceramic swan T.V. lamp. 12". $75-100

Brass rooster lamp with laminated scenery shade. 31". $50-75

Plaster oriental lamp with venetian blind shade. 16". $150-195 pair

Ceramic junk and Chinese couple T.V. lamp. Venetian blind shade. 19". $75-100

Ceramic Chinese people in junk, T.V. lamp. Silk shade. 20". $60-75

Plaster gondola T.V. lamp with fiberglass shade. 10". $60-75

Plaster oriental T.V. lamp with plastic shade. 10". $50-75

Ceramic oriental lady lamp/planter. 12". $45-60

Plaster table lamps. Silk shade. Oriental man and woman. 38". $150-175 pair

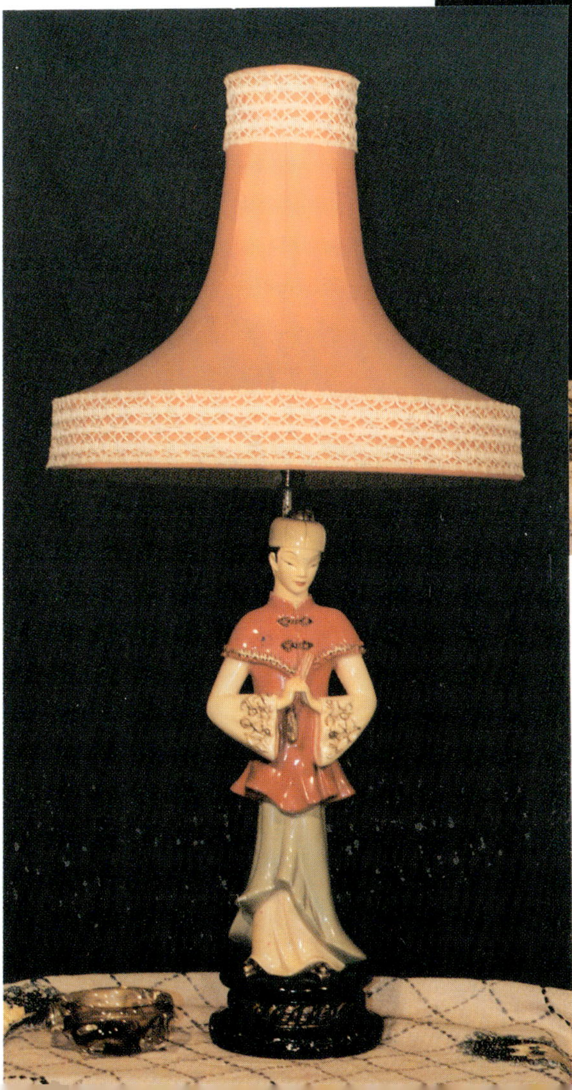

Pagoda planter base lamp. Cold painted on ceramic with cotton shade. 27". $50-75

Plaster Siam man, one of a pair, woman not shown. 18". $95-110 pair

Plaster dancing Hawaiian woman with chenille shade. Continental Art Co. 1951. (Came with a male dancer also) $300-600 pair

Wooden aloha table lamp. Red lights in breasts. 19". $100-175

Chalk oriental dancing man and woman table lamps with silk shades. $300-600 pair

Hawaiian woman in boat, T.V. lamp. Ceramic with gold splash paint. 8". $75-150

Plaster Polynesian woman, T.V. lamp. 13". $100-150

Plaster male dancer table lamp. Came as a pair, with male and female lamps. $175-225 pair

Plaster African mask T.V. lamp. 20". $75-100

Plaster Blackamoor table lamps. 22". $100-200 pr.

Blackamoor plaster T.V. lamp with silk shade. $100-150

Plaster Blackamoor table lamp with fiberglass and fabric shade. 16". $50-75

Wood and Lucite lamp with ceramic Blackamoor and silk shade. $65-100

Animated, Motion, and Clock Lamps

Electric metal lamp with glass insert. Fish swim around clock. 8". $150-200

Pot metal hula woman table lamp with clock insert. Burlap shade and fringed skirt. 22". $400-800

Bakelite and glass neon clock/night light. 6". $200-300

Pot metal hula woman table lamp with clock insert. Burlap shade and fringed skirt. 22". $400-800

Lava Lite (Aladdin-style), brass and wrought iron. Phased out in 1977. 14". $75-100

Waterfall scene, motion lamp. Metal with plastic shade. 11". $125-150

Brass Lava Lite with original box. Century Classic. Circa 1965. Still being produced today. 17". $75-125

Glass and brass Lava Lite. Flower ring. 16". $50-85

Ceramic bulb-style lamp and clock to match. Clock: 7.5"; lamp: 12.5", $100-125 pair

Ceramic bird set lamp. Lights up from back. 22". $100-150

Ceramic clock lamp with venetian blind shade. 26". $85-125

Floor Lamps

Iron floor lamp with African mask (different face on each side) in center. Fiberglass shade. 58". $200-350

Double fiberglass shade, metal floor lamp. 60". $200-350

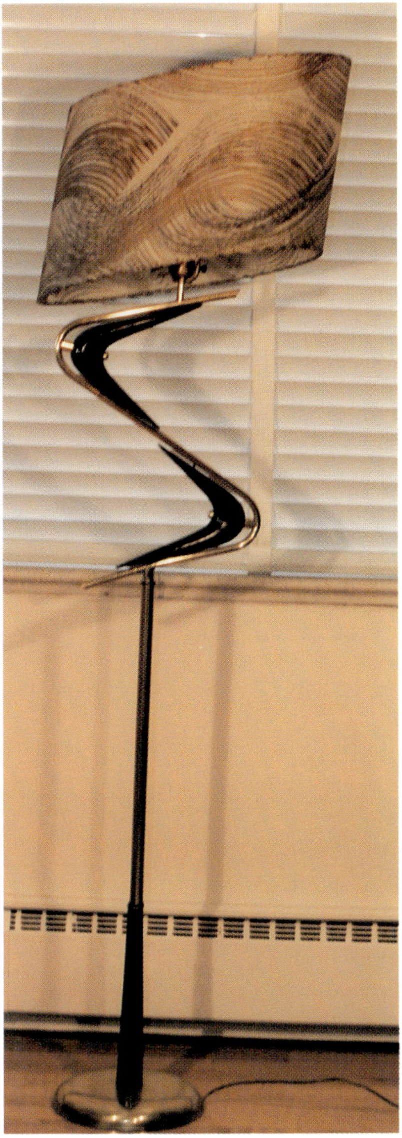

Swirl design brass floor lamp with fiberglass shade. 67". $200-400

Metal leaves on circular globes with twisted pole stem, floor lamp. Metal shade inside. Planter/lamp. 60". $75-150

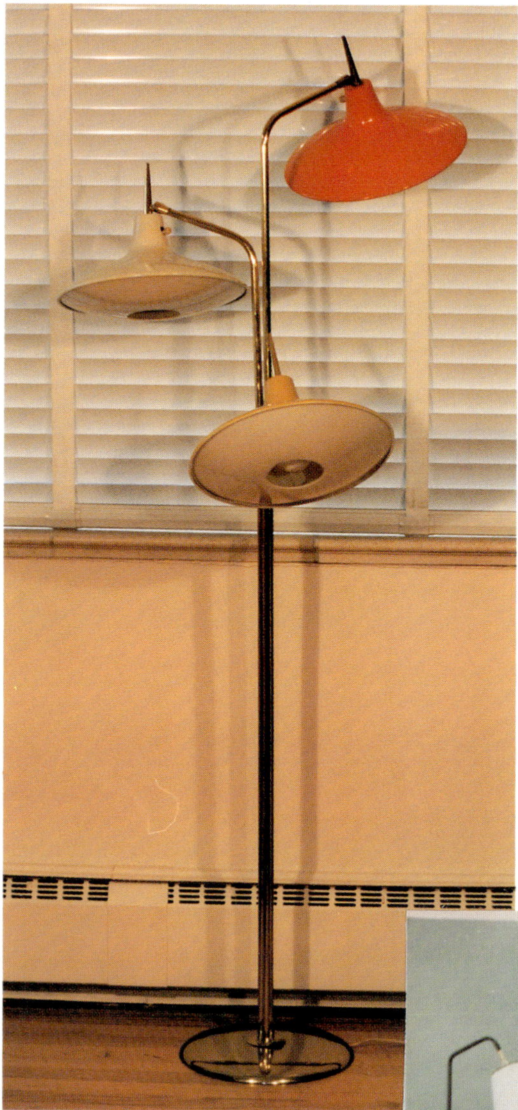

Metal floor lamp with disk shades. 65". $200-350

Left to right: Four in one combination wrought iron lamp. Ash tray, magazine rack, table and lamp. 50". $75-100. Double goose neck brass plated trim on base and bullet shades. 61". $75-95. Tole floor lamp with metal leaf decorated shade. 61". $40-65. Goose neck brass floor lamp with linen shade. 18". $35-60. Top Value stamp catalog product numbers shown. 1956.

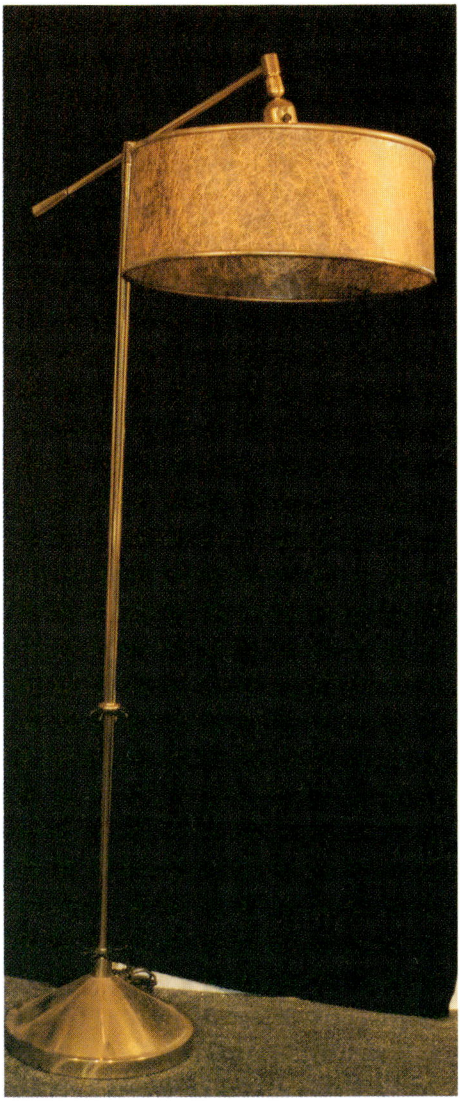

Brass and wrought iron floor lamp. Fiberglass shade. 60". $60-80

Brass and metal floor lamp with fiberglass 2 tier fiberglass shade. 60". $125-150

Brass floor lamp. Fiberglass shade. 60". $60-80

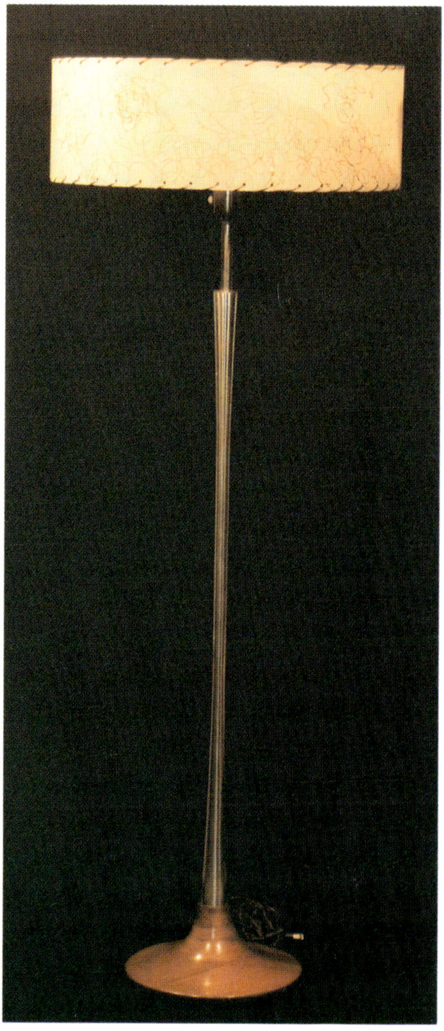

Brass and wood base floor lamp. Fiberglass shade. 60". $75-110

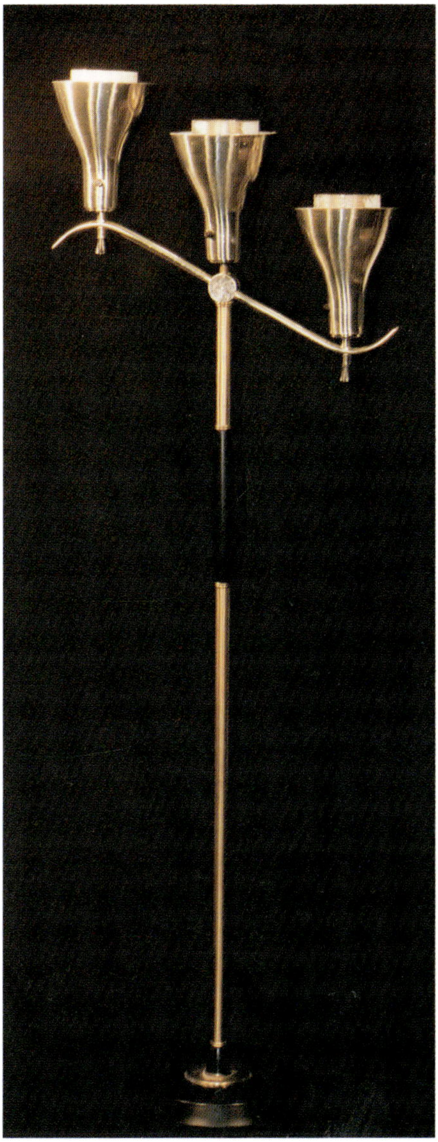

Brass and iron triple shade floor lamp. 60". $100-125

Brass starburst floor lamp. Fiberglass shade. 60". $125-150

Brass and ceramic floor lamp. Fiberglass shade. 60". $100-125

Metal floor lamp with 2 spotlights and 2 tier fiberglass shade. 60". $100-125

Bamboo and brass floor lamp. Cloth shade. 50". $100-125

Brass floor lamp with glass circular globe. This came as a set of 2 table lamps and 1 floor lamp. Rembrandt Masterpiece Lamps, 62". $275-375, 3 piece set. The table lamp mate to this piece is on the following page.

Brass table lamp. Rembrandt Masterpiece Lamps.

Brass and glass pole light. 8". $75-100

Metal bullet shape lamp. 60". $75-100

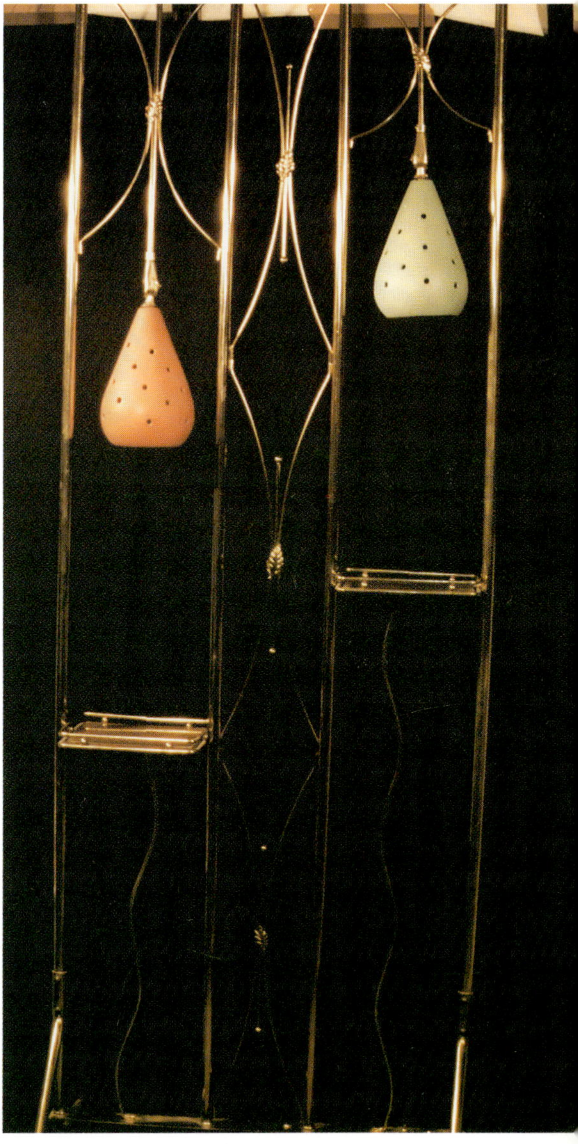

Metal wall divider lamp and shelves. 76". $125-175

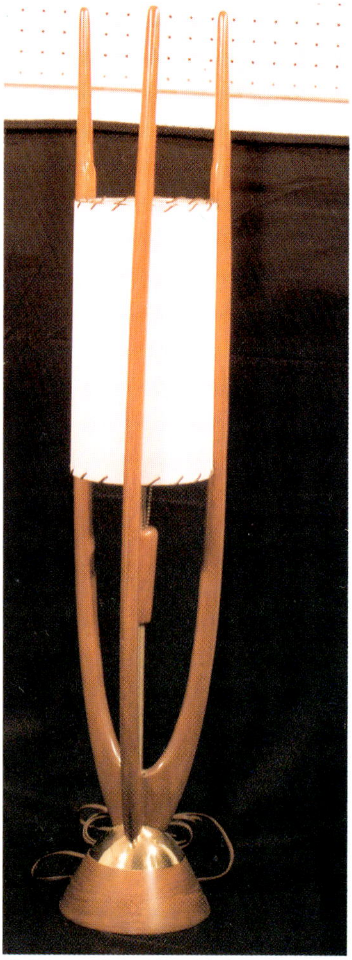

Wood table lamp with shade in center. 40". $100-125

Fiberglass triple globes on stainless steel poles, floor lamp. 60". $100-125

Hanging and Wall Lamps

Plastic grapes hanging light. 14". $30-60

Plastic grapes hanging light. $30-60

Fiberglass globe hanging light. 10"-12". $60-100

Milk glass hanging light. 12". $75-100

Wood and brass hanging light with triple plastic globes. $50-75

Newspaper advertisement for Lampland, Long Island, New York, featuring two styles of hanging lamps.

Glass teardrop hanging lamp from Finland. 14". $50-75

Red glass globe hanging light. 14". $30-40

Glass tube hanging light. 18".
$70-140

Spun fiberglass hanging ball light. $50-75

Green moon rock design, hanging lamp. 14". $40-50

Gold flecked hanging tear drop lamp. 12"-14". $50-80

Spun fiberglass/plastic globe hanging light. 10". $75-150

Wrought iron pin up lamp. Jet black mesh with parchment shade. 10.5". $30-40. Top Value stamp catalog, number 22-2. 1956.

Polished brass planter lamp. Linen on parchment shade. 10". $30-40. Top Value stamp catalog, number 22-3. 1956.

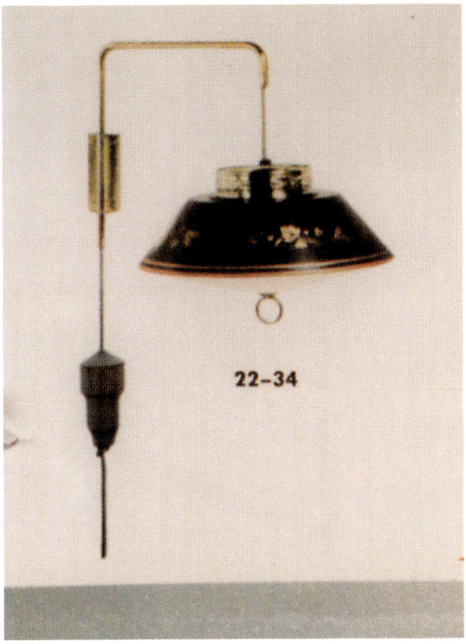

Adjustable polished wall lamp. 15". $45-75. Top Value stamp catalog, number 22-34. 1956.

Polished brass arm and hood with plastic reflector. Schrader. 13.5". $45-75. Top Value stamp catalog, number 22-47. 1956.

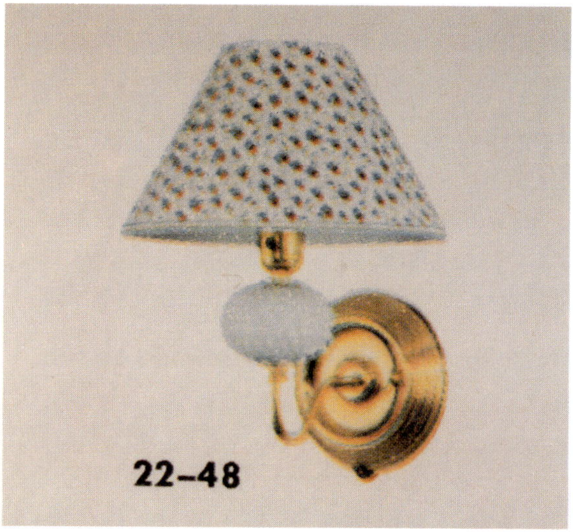

Hobnail milk glass and brass pin up lamp. Rosebud parchment shade. 8". $30-40. Top Value stamp catalog, number 22-48. 1956.

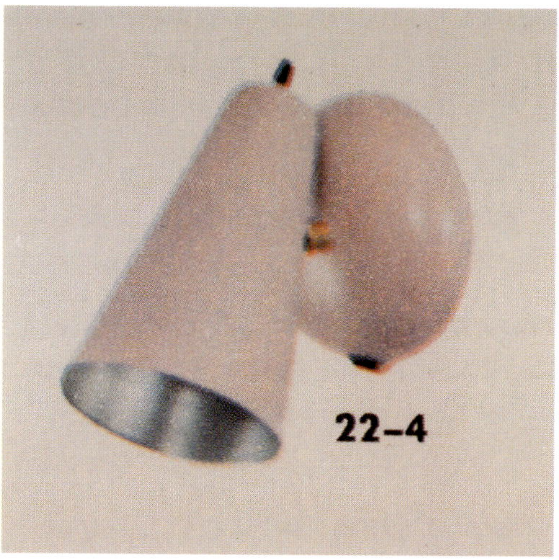

Metal adjustable shade and base pin up lamp. Extends from wall. 8". $20-30. Top Value stamp catalog, number 22-4. 1956.

Desk and Dresser Lamps

Metal phone/clock/ table lamp with venetian blind shade. 15.5". $175-200

Metal phone/clock/lamp. Metal shade. $75-100

Metal desk lamp. $40-60

Metal desk lamp. 14".
$40-80

Flying saucer coppertone desk lamp. Came as a pair. 16".
$75-125 each.

Desk lamp. 12". $50-85

Fiberglass table lamp with double shade. 24". $300-500 pair

Ceramic bulb base table lamp with metal half moon trim. 10". $30-60

Metal and brass dresser lamp with fiberglass shade. 12". $45-65 pair

Brass desk lamp with fiberglass shade. 15". $40-75

Brass adjustable desk lamp with parchment paper shade. 18" tall. $40-70 pair

Swing arm desk lamp. Brass with white boucle over parchment paper shade. Schrader. 18". $35-65 number 22-46. 1956.

Brass tube table lamp with floral fiberglass shade. $50-75

Pair of white glass bedroom lamps with hand painted roses on base and globes. 14". $50-60 pair.

Lucite and metal double table lamp with plastic shade. $60-75

Grecian urn lamp. Brass base. 9". $30-50. Top value stamp catalog, number 22-16. 1956.

Table lamp/planter. Brass base with fiberglass drum shade. Schrader. 25". $40-50. Top Value stamp catalog, number 22-49. 1956.

Brass and copper lamp with metal shade and frosted chimney. 15". $30-40. Top Value stamp catalog, number 22-14. 1956.

Polished base and shade holder. Milk glass shade with star design. 11". $30-40. Top Value stamp catalog, number 22-10. 1956.

Colonial, brass trim hobnail glass table lamp with clear glass chimney. 17". $50-70. Top Value stamp catalog, number 22-13. 1956.

Set of boudoir lamps. Milk glass fount and base with polished brass trim, lumarith pleated shade, bow trim. Norman. 17". $50-75 pair. Top Value stamp catalog, number 22-43. 1956.

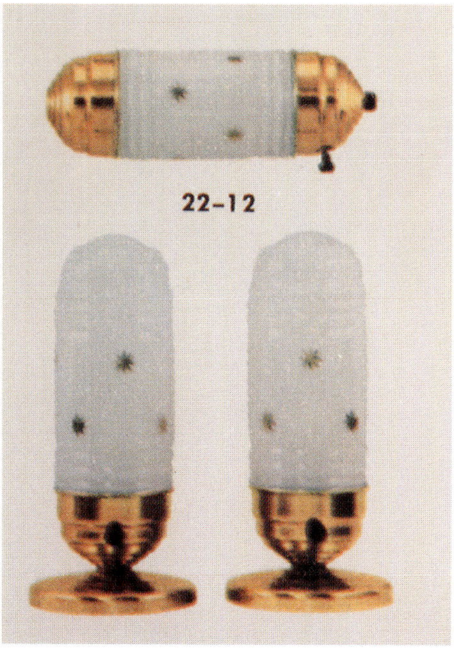

Vanity lamp set polished brass base with milk white glass globes. 3-piece set. 9.5". $85-125. Top Value stamp catalog, number 22-12. 1956.

Miscellaneous Lamps

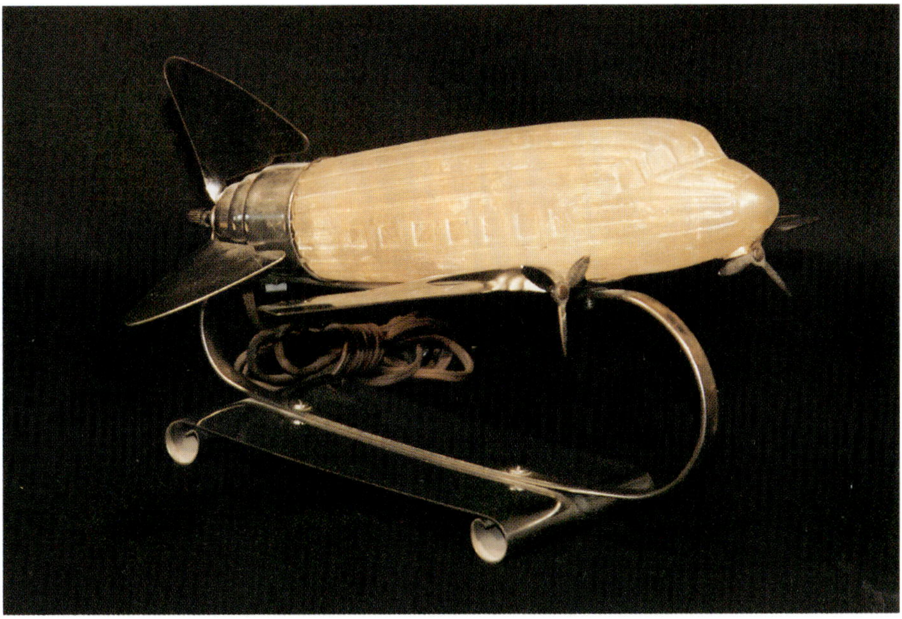

Frosted glass and chrome airplane lamp. 7". $350-550

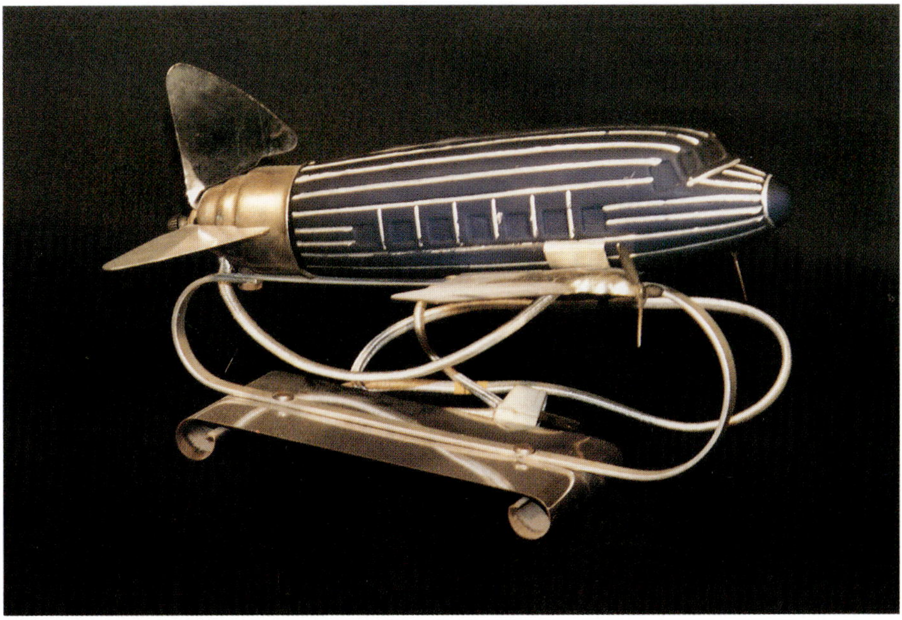

Frosted cobalt glass and chrome airplane lamp. 7". $350-550

Pot metal Statue of Liberty lamp. 11". $60-80

Copper lady holding vase table lamp. 17". $150-275

Green depression glass Saturn table lamp. $400-600

Green depression glass frosted Saturn lamp. $400-600

Van Briggle. Egyptian Goddess table lamp with plastic double layered shade. Artist Bill Higman. 1946-1956. $750-850

Ceramic mammy wall lamp with silk and plastic shade. $150-200

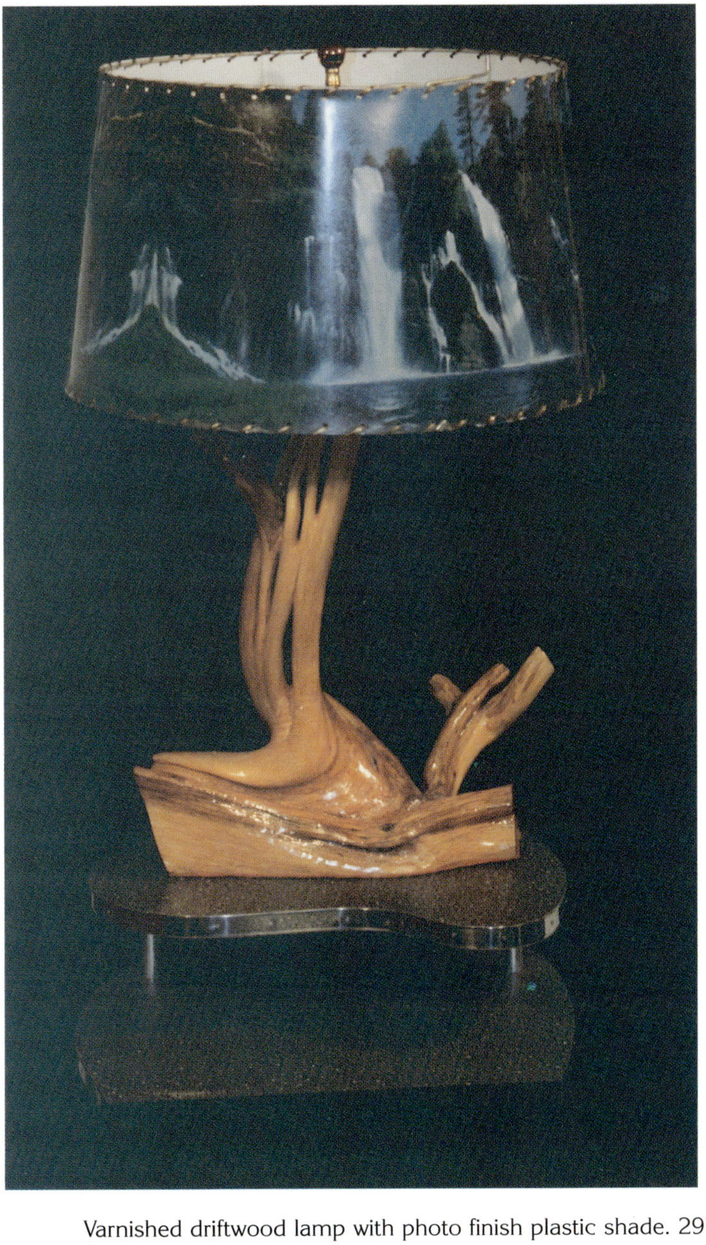

Varnished driftwood lamp with photo finish plastic shade. 29".
$125-175

Driftwood lamp shaped like a water pump with plastic western shade. 13". $60-85

Cactus wood table lamp with photo finish shade. $60-85

Glass bedroom dresser lamp. 10". $45-60

Green fiberglass globe shaped lamp. Cloth shade. 29". $30-40

Plastic candle lamps. $70-100 pair

Celluloid standing soldier light.
$50-80

Glass pineapple shaped table lamp. 11". $30-60

Cork table lamp with paper shade. 21". $40-60